Interactive Preaching

Opening the Word then Listening

Tim Stratford

Vicar of the Good Shepherd
(a large outer estate parish in the Diocese of Liverpool)

GROVE BOOKS LIMITED
RIDLEY HALL RD CAMBRIDGE CB3 9HU

Contents

The **Cover Illustration** is by Peter Ashton

Copyright © Tim Stratford 1998

First Impression January 1998
ISSN 0144–1728
ISBN 1 85174 363 4

1
Introduction

The suffragan bishop was presiding at my church's Confirmation Service last year. He went into the pulpit and began his sermon. After opening with a rhetorical question, the congregation started to answer him back. This surprised the bishop but seemed quite normal to the congregation who are used to talking to the preacher and respond poignantly to open questions. The Bishop recovered and carried on, being careful not to pause for too long after other pieces of rhetoric.

This book seeks to explore the value of congregations giving voice to their reflections on God's word during the 'sermon.' It is written after a personal history of priestly formation in Oxford and formative years in ministry spent at two large parish churches in the Liverpool diocese. A style of preaching was expected, learnt and exercised relatively uncritically in these contexts. To a reasonable extent it worked. People engaged with the sermon, and whilst being uncritical of the genre of sermon style were by no means uncritical either of the contents or delivery. These were good days of stretching development. Preaching was generally a very rewarding ministry, though on a bad day it could be more than a little dry and disheartening.

Then came a phase of ministry outside of parish life and an honorary curacy in an inner city UPA parish which was negotiated as a way of my keeping earthed.

Imagine a first sermon in this new context. The contrast of contexts has led me to a very different understanding of what the preaching slot in our liturgies can be about and that has led to this booklet.

Under the pressure of a new job and wanting to make a good impression on a new church an old sermon was drawn out of the cupboard—a good one, one that had led to much encouragement on a previous occasion. It was reworked a little and adjusted slightly to the new time and place it was to be preached in. There was no pulpit in this church, nor a congregation of hundreds rowed in pews, but there was a lectern behind which to take refuge with my notes at a safe distance from the twenty or so varied souls sitting in a semicircle and the few children playing on the floor in the middle. The sermon was delivered well, judged by previously inherited criteria, but it left no apparent impression—just glazed eyes and a slightly dazed looking congregation at the end of twenty minutes. Yet it had worked so well in other places.

The years that have followed have further highlighted the shortcomings not just of using the same sermon twice, but of a whole swathe of inherited formulas belonging to other times in the past and cultures far different to those of today's western Urban Priority Areas (UPAs). Academic didactic approaches using linear arguments or exposition from biblical texts and illustrations springing from personal experience forged outside the UPA context or from an agrarian past speak only to those who have learnt to digest this style. But many others are left completely cold or untouched by this and their own experiences and critical faculties may well alienate them from the church through it. Indeed even for those who can digest the lecture style there may be a better way to open up the gospel afresh.

This booklet will try to outline a particular alternative that has proved very rewarding and releasing, certainly to the preacher but apparently to church congregations as well. The experiences of dryness at the study desk pouring over pages and asking, 'What shall I say?' have gone; preparing for a sermon has now become a far more creative exercise of asking, 'How do today's Bible passages connect with the people here in a way they might be able to voice?' The preacher no longer needs to draw up four or five illustrations or a story or two to help people connect with God's word from reserves that he or she might find sometimes exhausted. And the congregation in sharing the responsibility can tremendously enrich God's word beyond the preacher's immediate ability, so enriching and affirming themselves.

Preaching in dialogue is more than asking questions, it is about engaging the congregation in a conversation. Where the preacher controls the answers to the questions there is no conversation. This is about risking real encounter.

It has been argued that the best of traditional preaching is in fact dialogue not because people talk back but because they interact throughout with what is being said in their own minds.[1] If this were so it would be a very unequal dialogue.

Preaching in spoken dialogue with the congregation rather than in monologue to them has certainly brought a new life and vibrancy to a flagging part of the liturgy in churches where a more traditional sermon style has never really worked. Hopefully this will serve as an inspiration to those with responsibility for opening God's word during worship in other, different, contexts to break the mould in ways appropriate there.

I am indebted to the people of St Bride in the City, Liverpool, and the Good Shepherd, West Derby, Liverpool for helping me along the road I am on.

1   John Stott, *I Believe in Preaching* (London: Hodder and Stoughton, 1982) p 60.

4

2
What is the Sermon?

Sermons happen only in religious meetings. Most people's expectations of what a sermon is might include its being delivered from a pulpit and its being based on Scripture.[2] Surely the heart of it is that the sermon is essentially part of the church's liturgy in which God's word having been read can be more deeply reflected on and retold for the here and now.

The preacher's kindred professions in the wider world might include the dramatist, the journalist, the social commentator, the novelist, the statesman, the poet, the playwright and the radio or TV producer.[3] Over the centuries that some of these disciplines have existed there has been a great deal of cross-fertilization and even more recently some of the multi-media disciplines are also making their mark on the practice of preaching. Preaching styles have gently changed with changes in culture and expectations from even thirty or forty years ago would not be met in many churches today.

Members of the congregation in one Liverpool church still reel in shock at the memory of a curate once riding his bike into church for a Palm Sunday sermon to make his point. The event is remembered for the effect it created and not especially for the message it was meant to convey. At the time this simple illustration obviously felt like a very radical challenge to what should happen in a sermon.

But in truth these gentle changes represent very little. They certainly do not represent any serious analysis of what a sermon is: its retelling of God's word and how this belongs in worship and liturgy. Indeed riding a bike into church may have cut very raggedly through these issues rather than addressed them.

Teaching or Retelling God's Word

Preaching and teaching are often confused. It is reasonable to expect a teacher to have all the skill or knowledge necessary to enable, instruct or train a person in a particular field. It would be arrogant of a preacher to claim this for the whole of life. A better term than teacher might be 'coach.' Often a coach is responsible for encouraging in a discipline people who themselves may be even more proficient than their instructor. This too has its short comings.

There are moments for teaching in the church's life. It is questionable as to whether these times belong in the liturgy or worship when we come to open the depths of our spirits to the heights of God's.

The preacher surely is on the same journey alongside those with whom he or she ministers. In some ways the preacher may have developed his or her skills and knowledge beyond those of many in the congregation for their benefit. This

2   cf *Concise Oxford English Dictionary.*
3   Following John Stott, *I Believe in Preaching* p 39.

might be especially true of their historical understanding of the Bible and its times, the history of God's people and his church, academic theology and human pastoral sensitivity. But the people of a local church may well have a wider experience than the preacher in applying God's word to living in their neighbourhood and home, the joys and short-comings of their own fellowship, the hurts and encouragements of Christian witness in that culture. Whereas the preacher might be best expected to bring real insight from the wider church to bear, members of the local community might best express the daily significance of what that will mean for them there.

Preachers then, knowing their role in worship and place before the congregation, have a duty to see that God's word is presented openly and plainly enough for the people to reflect on how it challenges the way they live. This is real work. Although God can speak through the Bible to people with very little help from others, he speaks ever more clearly to us as we listen to a wider circle of minds that have known and assimilated his word.

Even communication across the most perfect of media is subject to confusion. One person speaking to another face to face may need to say something more than once for the other person to catch what is being said. Sometimes the mind of the listener may be occupied by something completely different to that of the speaker and it will gradually become clear that some clarification about context or subject matter is needed before the listener can latch on. Even in the world of high speed electronic communication noise creeps into the system and much 're-dundant' information must be sent to ensure that the real information is received undistorted. Sending and receiving information, speaking and listening, is an imprecise business. We should expect it to be no different when we are trying to hear what God's word has to say to us; the more perspective we can draw on to get the message the better and more transparent the message will be.

Preachers who are so single minded as to think that they have God's message to give to the congregation, and anybody else's perspective on it will be a distortion, are failing to notice their own human frailty and the deep spirituality and working of God in others. This is not to deny the validity of more traditional preaching styles but it does note how hard all preachers must try to listen to others' and not just their own consciences.

John Finney is surely right when he says, 'Because of the skew by which leaders tend to see things through their own eyes, the pulpit is seen as more important than the pew...Mission is primarily the action of God in the congregation, not the leader.'[4] That the preaching style takes notes of this observation is perhaps as important as the sermon contents.

The Liturgical Context

In his excellent book on the meeting points of Christian orthodoxy, liturgy and pastoral care, Robin Green describes worship as best understood in the light

---

4   John Finney, *Understanding Leadership* (London: DLT Daybreak, 1989) p 13.

of this combination of ingredients as a moment when 'His story meets our story.'[5] It is in this context that the sermon belongs and no other.

In his work in Brazil among poor communities Paulo Freire saw that they could become very much stronger if people's eyes were opened to read critically 'truths' that were too often received as givens.[6] The critical cycle he developed of 'Analysis, Deciding, Acting, Reflecting' has become recognized good practice in much work with communities who have otherwise been disconnected from the powers which shape their world and assumptions.[7] The worship of the church can also be helpfully understood in these Freirian terms:

- *Reflection:* those who offer themselves in worship week after week bring with them the burdens and joys of all that has happened in the previous days. In worship they enter God's presence reflecting on how their lives have been. This might be by using a confession near the beginning of the service, it might be through prayers of joy and praise like the Gloria. Maybe even the Collect for Purity serves this purpose, though inadequately.
- *Analysis:* they listen to God's word and through the action of their own minds and words spoken during the sermon will form an analysis of God's will.
- *Decision:* through prayer and perhaps sacrament expression is given to their desire for that will to be borne out in what they do.
- *Acting:* the dismissal bids that the people act as the God they have worshipped commands: 'Go in peace to love and serve the Lord.' A journey round the cycle is completed when they return again to conscious and corporate worship of God.

Such an understanding of the centrality of liturgy in the whole life of the worshipping community can have a transforming effect on the way that liturgy is used. Robin Green's bidding that the liturgy should connect with the real and earthy aspects of life in a particular locality takes on far more urgency. Yet there must still be place for the universal and catholic points in the worship which bond the church and give expression to our wider fellowship as this fellowship is also surely God's will.

There is increasing use of resources such as *Patterns for Worship* which give more scope to local development of worship services to meet particular perceived needs. This development is sometimes in tension with those concerned that catholicity is not squeezed out. But there is a core minimum of local creativity which nobody today questions: it is most widely expressed in the architecture of the place of worship (stained glass windows, plaques on the wall, colour and light); the prayers of intercession (encouraged by Series 3 and *ASB* in particular

---

5 Robin Green, *Only Connect* (London: DLT, 1987) p 132.
6 See Paulo Freire, *Pedagogy of the Oppressed* (Harmondsworth: Penguin, 1972).
7 See Ann Morisy, *Beyond the Good Samaritan* (London: Mowbray, 1997) for an analysis of how Freirian principles relate to church based community development work, especially chapter 5, p 61ff 'Grace through dialogue.'

and, with an even deeper degree of local authorship, to be encouraged even more strongly in Rite A Revised); and the sermon.

Priests, readers and other ministers educated and trained outside of the context they find themselves working in have clear responsibility to see that the interaction between His story and that of the people among whom they minister is genuine. Where the local church context is radically different to those where training colleges and universities are found there is an even greater burden on those who exercise a preaching ministry to be sure they do not assume too great a self sufficiency.

3

Cultural Shifts and the Challenges of Today

With the ascendancy in importance of the mass media, political leaders have quickly learnt that sound bites can communicate ideas and be retained by people much more easily than the contents of a long speech. The power of visual stimulation alongside talk has led to the importance of television as a medium. Television is just beginning to learn from newer forms of multimedia communication about the importance of interaction and digital, satellite and cable technology is just starting to make this possible. Radio producers have known about the importance of interaction for at least thirty years since the advent of local broadcasting and the phone-in programme. It is not so easy now to brush off the consequent changing expectations about the means for passing on messages or telling stories as it was when John Stott was writing in defence of traditional preaching styles.[8] Nor perhaps is it as necessary as it then seemed. To lose confidence in certain limited modes of preaching is not the same as to lose confidence in preaching. Indeed many of the new understandings about communication and learning should help the church retell the gospel far more powerfully than it has been able to in the past. Some of these new understandings must be applied to preaching as much as to other means of education and mission.

Reality and Wonderland
    The nature of the competition that the electronic mass media presents to those who try to communicate at the human face-to-face or neighbourhood level have long been realized. On television and in the new digital multimedia sphere the boundary between reality and fiction is blurred. Colin Morris has argued that even where it is clearly sign-posted that television viewers are watching the real

8   *I Believe in Preaching*, pp 64ff.

8

thing, in their mind the boundary between fact and fiction is still vague.[9] On television the pace of events is very much faster—there is probably no street in the world that has had even one tenth of the experiences, hurts, pains, joys or arguments of *Neighbours'* Ramsay Street. The number one question a fiction producer will be asking about every scene is, 'is this believable?' 'Faction' programmes like *Crime Watch* or *999* straddle the boundary of fact and fiction. The power of personal computers lends even more power to blur this boundary in the new emerging digital multimedia market.

Bishop David Sheppard observed during the 1990 Broadcasting Bill debate in the House of Lords that society was now being lived out in the mass media. If this is true it could possibly be that some people feel they know Peter Sissons better than they know their own next door neighbour. The mass media and the electronic media are giving greatly increased significance to national and international events and 'personalities.' At the local level some communities are fracturing under a whole host of factors from economic oppression of the poor to the deep self-sufficiency of the middle classes. This helps a creeping loss of interest in the local neighbourhood, exacerbated because it is not on the agenda of those who illuminate the box in the corner of the living room.

Churches can either take these factors into consideration or condemn them but they cannot make them go away. Thank God that many Christians are ensuring that the gospel is kept alive in these new electronic communities where society is being lived out. The local church must find an answer too, giving localness significance once more and acknowledging the shifting codes of acceptable and good communication.

Other Realities

The competition that other media represent is only part of the story. There are other new facets to life in Britain and perhaps most of the western world which should challenge the way Christian ministers preach.

It is often said that the attention span of people today is not as long as it once used to be. This most often seems to refer to people's ability to listen to somebody for long periods of time. A media studies teacher in Liverpool tells his students that no television shot should remain still for more than two seconds as the viewer will get bored with the image. It is unlikely that these observations represent real changes in the capacity of people to give attention *per se*. Many people do give attention for very long periods of time in motorway driving, routine office work, and time spent on a production line for instance. People's ability to give attention depends heavily on the degree to which a high level of arousal is achieved. This may be provoked and maintained longer by occasional fresh stimuli (like ringing telephones or flashing lights) or may be achieved with slow decrement by a high significance to the individual of what they are attending to (like driving at 80mph

---

9 Colin Morris, *God in a Box* (London: Hodder and Stoughton, 1984) p 41.

along the M6).[10] A number of preacher's techniques, like the use of visual aids, try constructively to employ the first of the psychologist's observations. This might betray an assumption that a low significance to the hearers of what is being said is assumed. Better surely to work at the significance of the 'sermon.'

It is certainly true that many more people today are unused to what happens in a church compared with a number of generations before. The Willow Creek movement is one way of addressing this. It may well be that the newcomer who enters a church for one reason or another on a Sunday is somebody the preacher would most want to be speaking to. In most parish churches it will almost certainly also be true that such a person, along with finding the liturgy a little alien, will not have experienced being talked to for an extended period of time in a monologue from on high. If so they may be very ill-equipped and unprepared to hear what is said no matter how vital that is.

The 1960s saw a marked increase in the rejection of formal authority. Many felt that this was no different to the rebellion of previous generations of teenagers. Yet today the idea of deference has clearly been eroded right away as was never envisaged then. Add to this a 'pick & mix' trait which may well be part of a new emerging postmodern culture. This is borne out in contemporary art as much as in attitudes and behaviour. In such an environment, if the foundation the church tries to stand on is its authority as the house of faith or its insistence that it has the only valid interpretation of God's word to the world, it will find it is in a swamp. A far more open and dialogical approach, rather than authoritarian or didactical, might bring it again the firmer ground of credibility.

John Hull is an educationalist and Senior Lecturer in Religious Education at the University of Birmingham. In his analysis of modernity and the factors that govern Christian adult development today he isolates two factors as key to promoting Christian maturity and responsibility:[11] the one who teaches is not to be thought of as superior to the one who learns as learning can happen both ways;[12] adult learners should be invited to become 'creative participants' in their own development and in the task of understanding and changing the world.[13]

Finally it is worth noting that culture is not homogeneous. Whilst there may be common points that all preachers should know about the nature of human interaction today, there may be deep contrasts in values between one place and another. Canon Neville Black, a senior priest in inner city Liverpool, has long pointed at some of the deep contrasts between the values of working class Liverpool cultures and their neighbouring middle classes. For instance:

- among the weekly paid living is more day to day, flexible and hand-to-mouth whereas among the monthly paid frugality and long term financial planning

10 See for instance Ernest Govier's paper in Radford Govier (ed), *A Textbook of Psychology* (London: Sheldon Press, 1980).
11 John M Hull, *What Prevents Christian Adults from Learning* (London: SCM Press, 1985). See especially chapter 5, 'Jesus Christ, God and humanity: partners in learning.'
12 *op cit*, p 236.
13 *op cit*, p 237.

are valued;

- in working class communities the corporate sense is treasured, historically borne out and expressed through unionization or the common landlord of the corporation whereas among the middle classes individuals are encouraged more explicitly to stand on their own two feet;
- education is valued highly by the middle classes, earthy wisdom by the working classes;
- the working classes use an elaborate verbal code with a large vocabulary when they speak, in working class Liverpool 'yes' can mean 101 different things depending on how it is said.

He uses this analysis as an answer to those who want to argue that different class cultures do not exist. Call it what you will, differences exist across broad characteristics which colour people's outlook and behaviour. Interestingly it is normally those termed by this analysis as middle class who want to argue that such cultural differences have disappeared in Britain today. Christian ministers who preach will also normally be middle class by virtue of the formation the church offers them before giving them authority to preach.

4

A Little Theology

This is what he showed me: the Lord standing by a wall with a plumb-line in his hand. 'What do you see, Amos?' Yahweh asked me. 'A plumb-line,' I said. Then the Lord said, 'Look, I am going to put a plumb-line in among my people Israel; never again will I overlook their offences.
                                                                                            Amos 7.7-8

Amos's message was that compared to God's measure, the way of his people the Israelites was crooked. As was suggested a little earlier, one of the strong features in the emerging cultural shifts that seem to be currently taking place is that those who claim authority, who thus suggest that their way is absolute and objectively right, will be at best questioned or at worst written off as irrelevant. The argument of authority as a means of proving right and wrong no longer stands up. This should not be perceived as a threat to the church nor to this subject of preaching. The sermon does not have to stand or fall simply on the authority of the church or preacher. But at the same time it is vital that the preacher does not lose the confidence of his or her roots, where they are coming from, the whole basis of life as it is that has brought them to minister as they are.

According to Paulo Freire, one of the marks of the frame of mind that helps in this sort of transition is deep humility.[14] In the terms of the Amos prophecy this means recognizing that the place in which you have been formed, its structures and traditions, may be crooked compared to God's absolute straight and perpendicular. There are other traditions, alongside the expression of church which is precious to us (in my case the bookish Anglican evangelical variety), which will also no doubt be crooked too but which may be as near to God as our tradition; which when viewed from within our crooked house may seem more crooked than they do when viewed from heaven. We have no grasp of heaven's straightness but in remembering our crookedness we may be a little more reticent to judge others harshly.

But every one of us needs our framework in the here and now to give shape to our own lives. Our own crooked building is the best we have got, even if it is crooked. Amos's prophecy to 8th-century Israel offers us the confidence that God's objective perfection is not tied to our crookedness as it was not tied to the religious structures then. Other expressions of church may yet be developed that are quite different from what we know but nevertheless as godly. The humility in the preacher that gives space for surprising alternatives to find voice also forfeits the control to force the church into the mould of the preacher's own personal formation—and it may well release the people of God to bring something more appropriate to birth. It is undoubtedly true that in many UPA communities, as undoubtedly in other places too, most of the current expressions of church and theology have struggled.

Dialogical preaching is a step along the way by which control of theology and ecclesiology dominated by one culture can accessibly be offered to others. In some communities this is not just an issue about effective communication but also about control, justice and releasing Christian people from the bonds of a middle class culture which does not connect so well with their own environment and neighbourhood.

An exacerbating factor in our clinging to the expression of church that has nurtured us can also be a faulty understanding of doctrine and the history of its development.[15] Every step along the way doctrinal development has been by the action of human minds on the questions of the day. All doctrines, as we might now term the results of this process, belong to particular times and places. Some are relevant to the present and some are not. Those that are not, the church usually finds a convenient way of forgetting. But doctrinal development has surely not stopped. Nor, surely, is it confined within the bounds of a particular sort of academic questioning.

Priestly and ministerial formation can encourage its subjects into believing that part of the duty is to carry the wealth of received Christian doctrine as it now stands to places where it may not yet have reached. It is important that the way

14 See Ann Morisy, *Beyond the Good Samaritan*, p 67.
15 John Hull develops this point well in the last two chapters of his book, *op cit*, p 149ff. Memorably he says, 'The wings of suprise have been clipped by those who want to make the bird of heaven inhabit an aviary.' p 223.

doctrine has developed is opened up before all God's people but it is just as important that they can see they might have a role in its continued development where they are. Each context has its own particular questions to ask. In coming to terms with these questions local churches are engaging in just the same process that has led to the creation of doctrine, much of which we consider to be so precious. This creativity must surely not be stifled by the need to receive all the givens of every previous generation first. How can the church possibly address some of the unaddressed questions of today's society, especially some of the most down-trodden places, if the people who live there are not given space to join in this process?

Not every doctrine formulated has been supra-contextual. Some appear as if they are. It is not wrong that doctrines belonging to the particular times and places of today are given expression—and that they be named as such; not just good ideas but what being the church here or there is about, what God means here. The preacher can give space as much for this important work as for the rehearsal of the doctrines of other places.

Robert Schreiter has identified three ways by which theologies in a new local context are developed.[16] The simplest of these is a 'Translational' model whereby symbols and imagery are translated in a manner akin to dynamic-equivalence methods of translating the Bible. The second he terms an 'Adaption' model whereby the culture is analysed by those who bring the message first and then its own patterns are reinterpreted in the light of the gospel.[17] This is as much pagan ceremony and symbolism has been reinterpreted through our own church's history. He offers a preferred third 'Contextual' model which begins with the needs of a people in a concrete place: 'How is a Croatian refugee to live in New York City? or an African immigrant worker in Berlin?'

Many who preach will not see that there is an issue they must address here. They believe that for many layers of British culture the gospel has already been contextualized and in some places they may be right. But in places where there is a general sense for most that the gospel has no relevance then the church cannot sit back quite so comfortably. Here especially the mode by which the gospel is applied in preaching (as in other aspects of the church's life) must be considered.

16 Robert J Schreiter, *Constructing Local Theologies* (London: SCM Press, 1985).
17 For a good example of this model see Vincent J Donovan, *Christianity Rediscovered* (London: SCM Press, 1986).

5
The Practice

The Congregation's Stories

Many Christian ministers are well resourced and equipped to prepare their sermons in quite a self-contained way. Their theological and pastoral formation should have provided them with tools that help interpret the happenings around them both in terms of salvation history and in terms of human behaviour, good and bad. They will have nurtured a critical mind and might be capable of bringing deep insights to bear in the muddiest of waters. They are likely to have developed a great range of stories, both borrowing from other people and drawing on their own experiences, which help illustrate their theology and which will be filed away in a neatly ordered mind or preserved through a discipline like 'journal keeping.' Their shelves will be arrayed with joke books, dictionaries of quotations and Bible commentaries. Such and more have been the tools of the trade.

What a task the preacher sets him or herself. Many have to come up with the goods from their own store week after week. Sometimes the contents of the cupboard seem sparse and life is hard going for preacher and long-suffering congregation. Sometimes the cupboard is bare and there is a crisis of ministry.

Well there is another cupboard. Most churches contain within them a great wealth of experience as to what it means to live out the gospel in its community—far more living illustrations than ever the preacher's study shelves are likely to hold. The minister who finds a way to tap into this will also find a great liberation from the burden of being the only interpreter of the gospel. The members of the congregation may also be liberated from the mental contortions they have to make week after week to translate or adapt the preacher's experiences and illustrations to their context sometimes with the preacher's help, sometimes without. In opening this cupboard many of the theological and cultural questions considered so far are also addressed.

A proud element of Church of England ethos is that those who exercise priestly and diaconal ministries are sent to live alongside the people—the literal etymology of the word 'parish.' Nevertheless it would be arrogant for any ordained Anglican to assume that their experience of living in a place as a follower of Jesus would be the same as that of others, although in some cultural contexts it would be nearer than in others. Priestly formation, housing, security, recognition, focus of work and mobility all present strong differences. Tapping the wealth of experiences in the lives of the worshippers is far more than just a help to the preacher. Such experiences will be contextual and significant to that worshipping community from the start. The contribution that worshippers can make to the reflection on God's word which we call a sermon frees the minister and people from the need to translate or adapt life elsewhere to their place and provokes them instead to interpret life here in gospel terms as Schrieter demands.[18]

The preacher who can tap into local experiences of Christian living, being free from the burden of finding stories, translating and adapting their significance, is given space to learn more about the gospel's significance in that place. Such a continued personal development will enable him or her to make better use of particular insights and knowledge brought from the wider church. This is no licence to put centuries of learning to one side, but to bring it to bear more appropriately in the light of the new context. Nor is it a recipe to flounder because the received agenda has to be discarded, but to discover a new agenda of searching questions people are already facing and shed light on them.

The Nature of Dialogue

There are many more ways that those who have ministerial and leadership responsibilities within the church need to ensure they are contextually well rooted other than simply in how they preach, but in the liturgy we reflect much of what the church is about. If those parts of the liturgy which can give space and expression to the local context do not do so, the chances are that this reflection will be seen in the rest of the church too. The obverse can be argued too. If a church and its leadership collaborate or co-operate in day-to-day life and the big issues of direction and policies, yet this is not borne out in the liturgy, then why? The term 'an enabling ministry' has been very popular as a description of an able co-operative leader, but if the sermon is not 'enabling' and rather regards the congregation as receivers then this raises the question as to why there is a boundary point at which co-operation stops. Is the liturgy to be completely disconnected from the rest of life?

Since the growth of family services in the 1960s freedom of the congregation to play a part in sermons has been growing. It is important nevertheless to distinguish between times when the congregation is invited only to interact as a means of keeping them attentive and times when they are invited to interact as co-creators in re-forming the message. The terms 'open question' and 'closed question' offer a rule of thumb. For these purposes a closed question may be regarded as one which has a limited number of answers that may be regarded as right answers and for which other answers given might be regarded as wrong. A person who asks such a closed question might reasonably be expected to know what answers are permissible. An open question would be one which does not have wrong answers and which invites the questioned to lead the questioner on. For instance a language teacher might set for the class a comprehension test. The pupils are told a story about a bus and then asked questions about the bus which demonstrates the degree to which they understood the story. The comprehension test contains closed questions. Alternatively the same teacher might on another day invite the pupils write an essay asking them to tell a story about a bus; that would be an open question giving the initiative to the pupils.

18 See *Constructing Local Theologies* mentioned above.

Family service sermons most often contain closed questions and this may well be appropriate very often where children are the subjects of the questions. Although a closed question family service sermon bears similarities to dialogue, it should not be confused with it. Just because people are talking back it does not mean that preacher and congregation have entered into creative dialogue. This only happens when what is being offered back is more than just an answer the preacher may have already considered at the study desk but when the contribution made takes the sermon on further than the preacher could manage on his or her own.

The Mind of the Preacher

Preparing a sermon that relies on congregational dialogue may leave preachers who are used to having it all sewn up beforehand feeling very vulnerable. It may too leave them feeling as if they have not done their job properly and so perhaps strip their confidence. The consequent humility with which the preacher comes before the congregation will be no bad thing. The interdependence that is created between preacher and preached-to will itself say something about the church which is readily heard, understood and welcomed by many people today. Preachers also put themselves into a position where they can be changed or may learn.

None of this allows the preacher to shirk the responsibility he or she has for leading the people into a deeper appreciation of God's word. The preparation must be clear. The aim of contextually applying part of the Bible to the local church's own time and place is as vital as it ever would be for a didactic monologue. Preachers must still recognize their personal starting point and should not deny it. It is only from this base position that they can start to open God's word to the people, but having done enough to make plain this starting point and aim is all that is required. Pushing it home with three 'points' or some personal illustrations will deny the other people gathered the chance for creative dialogue or at best restrict them to a mimic of the preacher's view. Once the congregation have recognized clearly enough the relationship the preacher perceives between God's message to his people in the Bible and life today, they should be given space with judicious questions to take the sermon on. The preacher's duty is to echo back what is said so that all can hear, and to interpret what is said and make the connections the unprofessional speaker might have intended but not vocalized—always checking back with the questioner for assent. At the end the preacher will need to tie up the loose ends again. This tying-up can be prepared from within the preacher's own assumptions and the basis of where he or she has come from—but also leaving space to recall what others have said.

The Mind of the Congregation

Many people do not like to hear the sound of their own voice in public; others love it only too much. All should be released to share their insights. Alongside the preacher being prepared to enter into this dialogue, the congregation need space

16

to be prepared too and there is a learning curve that both congregation and preacher need to negotiate.

As has been suggested earlier, forms of preaching which allow congregational response seem to have an apparent growing cultural relevance. They are not the only valid form of preaching there is. Congregations seem quite capable of living with a varied diet. Use of the pulpit and a traditional preaching style together with Family Service closed question sermons still live happily alongside genuine dialogue. Indeed the variety will be appreciated in some places. Where there are members of a congregation whose traditional expectations make them unhappy with congregational responses to any form of question a varied diet may be necessary. Open question sermons work least well with family service congregations who normally expect children to answer questions with children's answers. Here there can be a deep reticence to offer significant adult answers which might only be overcome after a long period of discovery.

On any particular day it is probably enough that two, three or four people make significant contributions to a sermon. Some days the leader might be happy that the faithful contributors, ever ready to speak up, have their turn. On other days this may not seem right or timely; it could be that there are people who rarely speak up in the congregation who have particular understandings or experiences that are known about; it may be that a normally quiet member is evidently bursting to say something. There needs to be sensitivity on behalf of the preacher to where the congregation is up to.

There are a number of strategies that can be adopted to help, for instance:

- Closed questions during the preacher's introduction give an easy way for members of the congregation to hear the sound of their own voice before later making a more creative contribution. This is a stepping stone towards more significant contributions that the less obvious members of the congregation can especially be encouraged to join in with.
- Most often people will not want to get out of their seats or even stand up to contribute their thoughts. Do not put practical requirements in front of people that might crush their inspiration.
- Where the preacher knows of a member of the congregation's experience the person can be asked well in advance if he or she would be prepared to say something about it during the sermon. Such comments can even be given from the front rather than from the body of the church. This has something of the feel of a testimony being given except it is likely to be rather more focused than the story of coming to faith.
- The preacher might quite often have prepared a contribution to 'set the ball rolling.'
- It is not deceitful to provoke an ever ready contributor beforehand who might set the ball rolling but be open with the congregation about this: 'I was speaking to N before about this...'

Such 'sermons' also seem to need tidying up afterwards. This may be in prayer, it may be with a conclusion which the preacher has based on whatever contribution they planned to make but which also makes space for and recollects the other contributions from the floor. This is both simple and important.

In my experience, congregations challenged to co-operate in applying the gospel to themselves have shown a deep respect for the liturgical context in which they speak. The space is not normally abused. Contributions may sometimes seem a bit off-beam but gentle questioning by the preacher can often uncover where the contributor is coming from and the consequent self-interpretation may well be enough. Preachers do not need to be 'on their toes' in the way only a few entertainers ever manage. They do need to listen to what is said carefully, to be clear about the way their experience is touched by the word, and to be sure that whatever else is said connects too. This does not always mean making the connection—often it means trusting that the contributors know what they want to say but may need a little help in getting it all out. When and if the loopy is thrown in preachers need to remember that they are not on their own—others may be able to help out. Most will probably share the preacher's view about the loopiness too, and at the end of the day a comment like 'I guess most of us would not see it like that...' with nods all round is probably clear enough without feeling like a put down from on high.

The Physical Setting

The larger a congregation is the larger the job for stage-managing this type of sermon. With small numbers sat in a circle or horse-shoe no stage-management at all is needed. In a small church of less than a hundred and where the preacher can still stand in the nave or somewhere near the people the main problems are likely to be people hearing one another. A radio microphone can help but some find this intimidating. By encouraging people to face the centre of the congregation or repeating back to the people what is said every sentence or two when needed (and it will not be needed for every contributor) the problems can be overcome. The preacher certainly needs to be free to move to somewhere where he or she can best hear when a contributor is very quietly spoken. Sometimes other members of the congregation will echo back what is said well enough.

Once the congregation begins to creep much over a hundred it is very difficult for people to make spontaneous and sophisticated contributions without the use of a microphone. The size of the gathering may also itself become quite intimidating. The two most obvious solutions are to ask questions which do not require very sophisticated responses[19] or to prepare people well enough, maybe beforehand, to speak from the front. The chances are that such large churches will have quite sophisticated teaching and meeting arrangements outside of Sunday worship too. Co-ordination via these, perhaps with related issues being considered in the week and on a Sunday for the occasional short course, might help some mem-

---

19 See for instance the 'Ascension day' example in chapter 6.

bers of the congregation in an ordered way to overcome the hurdles of addressing a big church. This offers good opportunities for clear stage management which
saves the big church service from falling into chaos but the preacher needs to be
sure not to edit or filter too much what is to be said because of personal cultural
reasons.

Most churches will respond better to less demanding questions being asked
of them at early stages on the learning curve. As people get used to making significant contributions to the preaching so they will be more prepared to join in
with very ambitious exercises.[20]

It is possible to let the voice of the people be heard even in large cathedral
services. At a recent service celebrating ten years of the Church Urban Fund at
Liverpool Cathedral several local churches were asked to put up congregational
members with a prepared two minute script telling how they had engaged with a
particular CUF project. This formed part of the Ministry of the Word in that service.

_____

6

Example Outlines

Making space for a congregation to participate in the preaching of a church cuts
across perhaps just one or two traditions, though deeply ingrained traditions they
are. Breaking the habit of having a snooze during the sermon can be very shock-
ing for some; answering back to somebody speaking from the pulpit unthought
of by others. Liturgical and theological apologia need to be made by anybody
who challenges sacred traditions. The preceding chapters have attempted to do
this. On these few last pages are included four outline sermons which serve as a
real-life illustration.

These are sermon ideas that have actually been used in a number of situa-
tions. Where any have been used more than once the resulting sermons have
inevitably been very different. On each occasion I have come away more enriched
than I ever would have expected. I also believe that the congregation have connected more firmly with the word of God than ever they would if I in my voice
alone, with my own perspective and carrying my own set of cultural values, had
interpreted the Bible for them.

Church ministers can too easily carry around a sort of work ethic, believing it
is better to get lots of words down on paper and fill the allotted space than to
consider what those words are doing and how. Preparing an open space in which

_____

20 See the 'Parables of the Kingdom' example at the end of chapter 6 for the most ambitious form
of question this author has tried.

big questions can be asked fruitfully involves much more time spent dwelling on something than writing about it—thinking about the 'how' rather than the 'what.' The following examples try to give some sort of flavour of what can be added by the bountiful resources of God's kingdom people when they are released. This may serve as an encouragement to those preachers who worry about standing in front of a congregation without all their loose ends being tied up or perhaps even the whole sermon written down in front of them.

It is going to be a very exceptional church that adopts an open interactive style of 'preaching' exclusive of all other styles, though in places where there is normally a small congregation it is proving both sustainable and very fruitful. Much depends on the creativity of the preacher. A sermon which is going to communicate well needs an angle or key to it that will help people hold in their minds all that is said. Here at least I find something to agree with in John Stott's book.[21] Sometimes it will genuinely be much simpler to write a monologue than to beg open questions. That the example sermons offered have proved to be far more memorable to me than most of those entirely of my own authorship is in itself a testimony to the powerful way congregations are able to minister God's word to each other. For all sorts of reasons the full texts are not printed but simply an indication of where I was going and where the congregations went. In each case probably half of a twenty-minute slot was taken up with prepared material.[22]

All four involved a considerable amount of preparation. In some, such as Jacob's ladder, this involved a good degree of written preparation, both the history of Jacob's Bethel and the George McCleod story being quite involved. In others I seem to have done much less work. The first two examples offer a very structured approach. Although I asked questions where the answer cannot be predicted I was still in control of the shape of the sermon, its beginning and end. In the third example I gave permission to the people to interpret the Scriptures as they understood them. I may have disagreed with their interpretations and so would have to find a way to live with that. The fourth example demands a great deal of the congregation's creativity and without that a preacher would have very little left to develop—but people are often more resourceful than we think they might be.

Jacob's Ladder

The preacher's hope in reflecting on this story from Genesis 28 is that the people will find liberation to dream their own dreams rather than borrow other people's, and that they will find hope through God's fulfilment of Jacob's dream. Less significantly it might bring a powerful identification with Jacob as a fellow human traveller feeling for God's will and so help to demythologize a common Sunday School story. With a strong sense of place being carried by the story there is an assumption that the hopes and dreams the people are invited to recount will revolve around their hopes for the use of the church building—

---

21 John Stott, *I Believe in Preaching,* p 224—though much time has passed since this was written.

22 See Ernesto Cardenal, *Love in Practice: the Gospel in Solentiname* (London: Search Press, 1977) for a full record of a number of significant dialogical sermons.

assumed to be a real issue in the parish.

The following was prepared and used in two parts, to introduce and to close the space in which the congregation itself was given freedom.

Preparation

Examination of a Sunday School experience of telling the story reveals that all sorts of unimportant things can get in the way: The use of a stone as a pillow; prints of old master paintings which stay in the memory; the image of the ladder and the suggested location of heaven.

- Does that sort of telling of the story ring bells?

Brief space for the congregation to break the liturgical ice.

- Challenge to respond to the stories of the Bible as adults looking for real resonance with experience, rather than as with fairy tales:
  ◊ Our capacity to dream dreams and let them shape our lives.
  ◊ The importance of place in the story and its significance of Bethel to later generations.
  ◊ Hearing God's word and trusting his promises.

Substantial space is then left unstructured but questions help focus the beginning:

- What does Jacob have to say to you?
- What are your dreams?
- Are there places where you feel close to heaven or God?
- How might you respond to God's call?

The space having been carefully prepared to bring together God's words to us, the importance of location and our dreams, the intention was that the people would respond with dreams to develop the church. This sort of manipulation rarely works. The congregation had their own agenda and given the chance to talk about their dreams they did so.

In one of Liverpool's few remaining districts of real sectarian divide the dream that was recounted was of harmony and vibrant life between the denominations. The details do not need recounting. Capturing this energy from the congregation promised ecumenical change that had been preached about for many years but the surface of which had been barely scratched.

Conclusion

The Liturgy was then re-entered with a story from the preacher which betrayed the preacher's buildings-oriented agenda rather than the congregation's, but which nevertheless had value—with apologies and explanations to the people:

Iona stands as an entry point of the Christian faith to the British Isles. In recent times George McCleod played a significant part in the island's restoration and re-establishment on the spiritual landscape. This story itself gives a modern day connection with Jacob. This is most firmly grasped in George McCleod's words describing Iona as, 'a thin place—only a tissue paper separating earth from heaven,' but also borne in his dream for what Iona could be—both in stone buildings and in serving community...

21

Sacrifices—for Passion Sunday

The preacher's hopes here were to connect the feelings we have when we make small sacrifices for other people with what God was doing in the sacrifice of Jesus. In doing this we can discover a greater appreciation of God's love for us and can value our loving actions to others as echoes of our faith. The reading set was from Mark 10.

Mark describes Jesus' heading towards Jerusalem as very purposeful, done in the full knowledge of what was to become of him. At the very least Jesus could read the signs of the times and understood well the nature of human hearts; he understood the religious and political situation and readily acknowledged his unpopularity in some of the circles of power; he knew how fickle even his followers were. Even someone who accepts Jesus' divinity to have been totally laid aside for the sake of his incarnation can also accept that he headed towards his sacrifice in the knowledge of what he was doing.

The anticipated ice-breaker question was about the sort of sacrifices we sometimes make; the issue of substance for which there was to have been a more open space was about how we feel about some of the sacrifices people make. The assumption was that people would find it difficult to talk about their sacrifices. This was not to be. The sorts of sacrifices which had been anticipated:

- soldiers in war,
- caring for children,
- going to church,
- giving presents,

were small compared with the sacrifices actually shared by the congregation.

As in most churches this was a place where everybody knew each other at one level and yet did not at another. Here a daughter with her elderly mother regularly sat at the front. After one contributor's brief and shallow mention of the sacrifices parents make for their children this particular young woman told the congregation very movingly about the sacrifices a daughter might make for her mother without the possibility of the mother growing up and leaving home. The mother joined in the conversation and told of the frustrations from her side. This was a most moving experience. In its liturgical context this conversation was safe in a way that it might not have been anywhere else. It led others to open up with real experiences of sacrifices too. We never just heard from a soldier who had fought for king and country, but from a wife who had lost her husband fifty years ago and had never married again. There was no more incarnational entry into Passiontide than what this occasion offered. Later prayers of penitence and words of peace took on a new dimension across the congregation.

A safe conclusion that helped re-engagement with the liturgy, even though it was prepared in a relative vacuum, still had its place:

- There are different sorts of sacrifice:
  ◊ sin offering—by way of saying sorry, like a Temple sacrifice;
  ◊ duty;
  ◊ because of love;
  ◊ to achieve something better, like athletes or students;

22

Jesus' sacrifice rolled them all together. The Eucharist brings this alive for us.
And indeed it did.

Ascension Day

The preacher's hope here was to help the congregation into the lives of the disciples—
to appreciate the significance of Jesus' departure for them. This challenges the depth of our
love for him.

Here there is no 'closed' ice breaking question but the personal stories told right near
the beginning are reflected on again near the end in an attempt to make sense of the Ascen-
sion story. The question asked of the congregation is probably nevertheless safe enough
even to be used where this style of preaching is unfamiliar.

The Ascension is as final a good-bye as human beings ever have to make. All
of us have to say good-bye at times. Good-byes have given rise to a good many
classic images:

- an ocean liner leaving port amid streamers
- soldiers marching to war
- lovers on a railway platform
- gravesides

Space is then made for the people to talk around enduring memories of their own good-
byes. Stories that have been told do not need recounting here. Saying good-bye is a very
common experience right across the board. Stories told in this space were very moving and
very significant to those who had told them.

That actions speak louder than words connects strongly with our good-bye
stories. It is also true that saying good-bye to people leaves us with feelings it is
difficult to put into words. Jesus' disciples undoubtedly perceived something that
was greater than the limitations of the words they had to describe it. Just as our
accounts cannot always do justice to the good-byes we have made so we do not
always do real justice to the Ascension—we concentrate on the classic pictures
and not on what they tell us.

Space can then be made for the people to say how they relate to this story in the light of
their stories with encouragement to escape beyond the Sunday School images of somebody
heading upwards. Perhaps the preacher can contribute as an equal.

Parables of the Kingdom—Today's 'Sowers'

This is the most risky of the four examples given in that the preacher has very little
control over what might happen and is left with very little material of his own prepared,
very reliant on the congregation's creativity.

The hope of the preacher was to help the congregation into the everyday things that
Jesus drew his parables from and away from the idea that spiritual language must be
agrarian and foreign. Our modern urban lives too can be hallowed by God.

The congregation are to be warned right up front that they are going to be expected to
be creative and come up with a parable or two. It may be that logistics will be improved, if
this creativity is to take place in groups, by instructions also being given at the start. The
example recounted is drawn from the 'Sower' parable of Luke 8 and worked with people

thinking alone rather than in groups.

The congregation having been warned of the task that lies ahead of them are given an example of a 'sower today parable' to help them get the idea:

- Shoppers went out to shop
  ◊ some were unprepared and had no money
  ◊ some met other people on the way and did not get there in time
  ◊ some got attracted by all the luxuries and did not buy any basics.
  ◊ some had a fruitful journey and did not have to worry for the rest of the week.

To our contemporary ears this reads like just a good housekeeping story. It becomes much easier for us to see how the disciples heard his sower story as just a good farming story. Surely they knew there must be more to it than that, but they were perplexed until it was explained. The crowd never had it explained to them. What did Jesus leave them with? Some might have heard good sense, others perhaps the very much deeper truth.

The congregation might then be invited to describe their good sense parables. This has elicited a great deal of powerful material:

- *One young mum paraphrased the sower with herself and the work she needed to do around the house. The idea may perhaps have been developed from the first example given but her development of the things that got in the way was new and real:*
  ◊ *The baby crying*
  ◊ *The child who needed picking up from school*
  ◊ *The worry about not being able to get it all done*
  ◊ *The Hoover broke and it cost too much to repair*
- *Another came up with a parable of a journeyer who was travelling somewhere and much of what got in the way was their frustrations with other people and roadworks and train times.*
- *Another with learning to play the euphonium.*

Connecting these significant obstacles to day-to-day life with the things that get in the way of a life of faith can be fun and fruitful. Surely too it's a genuinely authentic way to interpret parables. Neither Jesus nor the Gospel writers develop academic treatises from them, but simply leave the everyday picture to endure, soak in and do its work. Those interpretations that are created by the congregations themselves are much more likely to speak back to them than are the interpretations other people invent for them.

Much of this connection-making the preacher may have to do on his feet—but the congregation can help with the connections when he's stuck! So we worked through each of the modern parables connecting the creative task with a spiritual challenge as the sower is often connected to an evangelist.

Finally to re-enter the liturgy again things should be brought back to order. The words of Jesus, 'He who has ears to hear, let him hear' sounds like a statement about the parable, but in fact it is his interpretation of it. Under the surface of all the created parables are lurking subtle forces that drown out God's voice and perhaps we need ears for this too.